CALIFORNIA COAST

CALIFORNIA COAST

CALIFORNIA COAST

PHOTOGRAPHY BY LARRY AND DONNA ULRICH

TEXT BY SANDRA L. KEITH

GRAPHIC ARTS CENTER PUBLISHING COMPANY, PORTLAND, OREGON

International Standard Book Number 1-55868-035-7
Library of Congress Catalog Number 90-71085
© MCMXC by Graphic Arts Center Publishing Company
P.O. Box 10306 • Portland, Oregon • 503/226-2402
President • Charles M. Hopkins
Editor-in-Chief • Douglas A. Pfeiffer
Managing Editor • Jean Andrews
Production Manager • Richard L. Owsiany
Designer • Robert Reynolds
Book Manufacturing • Lincoln & Allen Co.
Printed in the United States of America
Fourth Printing

This book is dedicated to our parents
who taught us early and wisely
how to love our natural world.

LARRY AND DONNA ULRICH

■ *Frontispiece:* Yellow tree lupines hug the hillside above Point
Reyes Beach in Point Reyes National Seashore. ■ *Right:* The gentle
windswept patterns on the Mussel Rock Dunes in the Nature
Conservancy's Nipomo Dunes Preserve glow in evening light.
At 450 feet, these are the tallest dunes on the California coast.

■ *Left:* Tidepools are revealed at low tide along the rocky shores of Channel Islands National Park. Afforded additional protection as a national marine sanctuary, the offshore waters of the islands harbor a great variety of deep-sea and intertidal creatures. Near Johnsons Lee on Santa Rosa Island, ochre seastars and purple urchins are exposed by a minus tide. ■ *Above:* A winter sun sets over Pebble Beach in Del Norte County. On Good Friday, April 13, 1964, a massive tidal wave—a *tsunami*—struck this beach and Crescent City, causing extensive damage on the city's waterfront.

conifers have existed for at least 160 million years. It was a prolific family that grew to encompass at least twelve species, and in the end their empire stretched across what is now Western Europe, Asia, parts of the Arctic, and most of North America.

But change was on the wind. As the Alps, Andes, Rockies, and Himalayas were thrust skyward, their lofty peaks cut off the humid sea winds which gave the trees their life. A drying trend set in, and as it did the moisture-loving conifers began to wane. And then the ice came, great, bulldozing sheets that entombed whole forests beneath their creeping chill. And when at last the earth stood fast and the icy death subsided, most of the giant trees were gone.

But not all. Far from their ancestral beginnings, in a place that would one day be called California, two red-wood cousins still raised their crowns toward the sun. The shorter, fatter relative, *Sequoiadendron giganteum*, lived only along the Sierra Nevada's western edge; the taller, slimmer cousin, *Sequoia sempervirens*, frequented only the state's north coast where winter rains and summer fogs sustained its titan form.

Today, the best of the best live within the boundaries of Redwood National Park. Here is the world's legacy of tall trees, forest monarchs that consistently grow more than three hundred feet high, with the king of them all topping out at nearly 370 feet. Their diameters are as much as twenty-two feet; their ages, in excess of two thousand years.

Individually, each tree is a mind-boggler. En masse, their presence is so overwhelming that onlookers tend to speak in whispers, for some of these ropy-barked patriarchs were young in the days when Christ walked the earth, stately colonnades by the time Columbus discovered America. Little wonder that in 1980 Redwood National Park was declared "especially worthy of saving for the good of mankind," and it was named by Unesco as a World Heritage Site.

Of the state's thirteen major tree communities, five grow along or near the coast. In those places where the fog flows heaviest, the redwood is often joined by Douglas-fir, Sitka spruce, and western hemlock to create mixed conifer forests that are impressive in their own

right. Equally interesting, though far from impressive, are the closed-cone conifers. Once widespread, these unusual trees are now relict species, for only during excessive heat, fire, or old age are their seeds released.

Although the closed-cone conifers freckle the coast between Humboldt Bay and Santa Barbara County, the most intriguing stands grow atop the eons-old marine terraces along the Mendocino coast. Their locations are scattered; their density, varied.

Yet along the Mendocino coast, all claim a common trait: they are pygmies. So is their accompanying under-story. Van Damme State Park has an excellent pygmy forest. So does Jug Handle State Reserve, along with Russian Gulch and Salt Point state parks. In any other place these trees would attain normal heights. But here, on this *podzol*, a word the Russians used to describe the ground's ash-gray color, the trees and their scraggly shrub associates have become a natural bonsai.

The culprit is the soil. Normal soil has a pH of 6.0 to 7.5. But where the pygmies grow, the soil has a pH of 2.8 to 3.9—about the same as vinegar. Besides being the most acidic soil in the world, *podzol* is devoid of minerals and organic matter—and if that were not enough, just a few inches below the surface is a hardpan so concrete that plant roots cannot penetrate it. So the feisty trees adapt. Here, the Bolander pine is biologically mature and pro-ducing fertile cones when it is only a few inches high; and the Mendocino cypress and bishop pines, many of which are fifty to one hundred years old, put forth fertile cones despite being less than two feet tall and having pencil-thin trunks a quarter-inch in diameter.

Although the Russians named the soil these Lilliputian trees grew on, they certainly didn't use them to build their fort on the Sonoma coastline. For that they employed redwood, and when the twelve-foot-high walls and the two double-storied blockhouses that surrounded their complex of stout buildings were finished, they named it Rossiya—an early form of the word Russia. In its time, it was the most heavily armed fortress on the coast of North America.

It was a plan that had been a long time in the making. By the end of the 1700s, the Russians had established a permanent settlement at Sitka, Alaska, and by 1799,

they had laid claim to everything as far south as 55 degrees latitude—now British Columbia.

By the beginning of the 1800s, Russian traders, acting under the czar's orders, had buried imperial markers that had been inscribed "Land Belonging to Russia" all the way south to San Francisco Bay. In 1803, the czar had dispatched Nikolai Rezanov, a career officer in the service of Russia, to scout out the coast of California for no other purpose than to see how strong the Spanish fortifications were.

After an extensive look around, Rezanov anchored in San Francisco Bay in 1806 and penned a report home. "If the Czarist government had given earlier thought to this part of the world . . . then one could positively maintain that new California would never have become a Spanish possession . . . today there is only one unoccupied stretch north of San Francisco, so useful to us and quite necessary, and if we should allow it to slip out of our grasp, what will posterity say?"

By 1809, Ivan A. Kuskov, chief deputy with the Russian American Fur Company, a semiprivate organization chartered in 1799 by Czar Paul I to control all Russian exploration, trade, and colonization in North America, was on the scene and ready to go. He scouted out Bodega Bay, which he christened Rumiantsev Bay, and by 1812 he had his official orders to build and govern a new settlement in California. And so he did. In March of the same year, he sailed his ship, the Chirikov, into a small cove just north of Bodega Bay and boldly took his party ashore. By September, the fort they had built was not only well armed, but vigilantly manned.

To all intents, they were there to stay. But it was not to be. By 1816, the sea otters, which they had so diligently hunted, were beginning to decline, and, by 1820, the settlement was more a food base for their Alaskan settlements than an otter hunting station.

But even their last hopes were dashed as the ever-present fog rusted the grain and a horde of hungry rodents ate most of what remained. In 1841, after failing to sell Rossiya to either the Mexicans or the Americans, the Russians struck a deal with John Sutter of Sutter's Fort in Sacramento. Within a few short months, they had packed their belongings and sailed away.

What they left behind is "one-of-a-kind." It is a little bit of Russia on American soil, and though it has been restored, refurbished, and—in some instances—rebuilt, it still stands atop the golden headlands where it was originally built. Today it is known as Fort Ross State Historic Park, and even though the Russian flag no longer snaps its staccato in the salty air, the fort itself is a reminder that from 1812 to 1841 this was soil claimed for Russia—a sort of Kremlin outpost at the edge of the New World.

There are a few other reminders along the north coast that the Russians were here. North of Ross is Russian Gulch, now a beautiful state park; south is the Russian River. The Pomo Indians who lived along this part of the coast called the river *Shabaikai*, Long Snake. The Russians named it *Slavianka*, Slav Woman. The Spanish, in reference to the Russians up at Ross, called it *Rio Ruso*. By any title, it is one of the north coast's prettiest and largest river systems and in its entirety drains fifteen hundred square miles.

The largest coastal rivers in all of California are in the northern part of the state. Easy to see why considering that the north coast receives 60 percent of the state's annual rainfall. Of all the California rivers, the largest is the Sacramento which, along with the San Joaquin and their many combined tributaries, eventually empties into San Francisco Bay. Second largest is the Klamath, and though it originates in the Oregon Cascades, it drains twelve thousand square miles to become an impressive waterway known throughout the state for its salmon and steelhead runs. Third in size is the Eel River which, when joined by its major tributary, the Van Duzen, fans out to form one of California's largest coastal wetlands.

Though the north coast abounds in pristine waterways, only a few of them are protected under the Wild and Scenic River Act: the Smith, Salmon, Trinity, Klamath, Eel, and Van Duzen.

Protected or not, the rivers and streams in this part of California are as spellbinding as the land through which they flow. And whether they glide past silent forests of fir and redwood or cut across timbered mountains by carving out steep canyons or simply meander lazily into the sea, all have one thing in common: they prove that, at least on California's north coast, wilderness survives.

Right: *Prairie Creek and Trail, Prairie Creek Redwoods State Park, one of the crown jewels of the State Park System*

■ *Left:* The wet climate of the northern coast creates the perfect environment for many varieties of water-loving ferns. Sword ferns, six feet tall, and lady ferns, gracing the borders of the rivers and creeks, are only a few. These five-fingered ferns, commonly found at Prairie Creek Redwoods State Park, are clinging to the banks of Prairie Creek while a horsetail stands guard at the other side.
■ *Above:* Boulders rounded by the constant battering of countless waves glisten in a winter sunset on Hidden Beach. The Yurok Loop Trail leads down to this beach, which is in Redwood National Park.

■ *Above:* The South and Middle forks of the Smith River join forces in Six Rivers National Forest before making the final journey to the Pacific Ocean. The river is named in honor of Jedediah Smith, who, in 1828, led the first overland expedition into the tangled forests of the region around the Klamath and Smith rivers. Famous for its transparent blue-green waters and its salmon and steelhead fishing, the Smith is California's last free-flowing river.

■ *Above:* The sulphur shelf, or *Laetiporus sulphureus,* is quite conspicuous among the greens and yellows of autumn in a redwood forest. Sometimes called "Chicken of the Woods," just the mere sight of one of these large fungi is sufficient to make a mushroom hunter's heart pound with delight. Not only edible but notably distinct as well, the bright orange, fleshy body is not easily mistaken for other fungi that may or may not be fit to eat.

■ *Above:* Beaches in this area change daily with the tides, weekly with the storm patterns, and monthly with the seasons. Currents, storm activity, and human interference can give a beach a whole new look. In winter, waves pull the sand from the beach at College Cove, part of Trinidad State Beach, making it a smaller, narrower beach than it is in summer. ■ *Right:* The northernmost reaches of California's coast get more than eighty inches of rainfall yearly, but snow is rare. This thin veil of snow below Split Rock in Redwood National Park lasted only a few hours before melting.

■ *Left:* Salmon berry and elderberry carpet the forest floor of Stout Grove in Jedediah Smith Redwoods State Park. The forty-four-acre grove, named for pioneer lumberman Frank D. Stout, was given to California by his family in 1929. ■ *Above:* Scattered like jewels on a green velvet pillow, the flowers of the Pacific Rhododendron are the stars of early summer in the coast redwood forest. As conspicuous and colorful as any rose, these magnificent blooms start in late May and last through June. One of the best places to view them is in Del Norte Coast Redwoods State Park.

■ *Above:* A string of prairies lines Bald Hills Road in Redwood National Park. Schoolhouse Peak, at 3,092 feet, is the highest point in the park. From here, views of Redwood Creek Valley and the distant coastline stretch out in endless panoramas. ■ *Right:* The Klamath River, second largest in California, has its headwaters high in the Cascade Range of Oregon. During the summer and fall months, the Klamath supports a large sport and Native American fishery. When the salmon run begins, the mouth of the Klamath can be so clogged with boats that to cast a line seems impossible.

■ *Left:* Anyone hiking in a virgin redwood forest can guess how Lost Man Creek was named. Ferns, fallen tree trunks and myriad blackberries, salmonberries, and thimbleberries give hikers the incentive to stay found. ■ *Above:* Yellow pond lilies flourish in sluggish Lagoon Creek in Redwood National Park. Small lagoons were formed in the last five thousand years by wave action and rising sea levels. This is a popular fishing spot, with picnic tables and access to the best spots to fish. ■ *Overleaf:* An unusual double rainbow arches over Luffenholtz Beach County Park near Trinidad.

■ *Above:* Stone Lagoon is one of three in Humboldt Lagoons State Park. When winter rains swell the stream that feeds the lagoon, the sand spit at the mouth breaks open, allowing the water to drain.

■ *Right:* The coastal community of Trinidad is considered by many to be the prettiest spot on the entire coast of California. The clean, uncrowded beaches, picturesque harbor, and spectacular array of offshore seastacks combine to help prove that point. Hundreds of sport salmon fishing boats converge to this area every summer, packing the harbor and trying their luck in the sea.

■ *Left:* The entrance to this sea cave can be reached only at extremely low tides. The view looks out at what is listed on official charts as Little River Rocks, but these prominent offshore seastacks are known to the locals as Camel Rocks because their shape suggests the animal's humps. When the swell is right and the surf is big, this is one of the most popular surfing breaks on the northern coast. ■ *Above:* This view is from Houda Point Beach at sunset.

■ *Above:* Western azaleas and Shasta daisies thrive in Azalea State Reserve, one of the northern coast's most beautiful natural gardens. ■ *Right:* Located in Eel River Valley, the entire town of Ferndale was designated a State Historical Landmark because of its Victorian architecture. Built in 1899 as a doctor's residence, the Gingerbread Mansion has become a bed-and-breakfast inn and one of northern California's most photographed Victorian houses. ■ *Overleaf:* Located in Kings Range National Conservation Area, Black Sands Beach is swept clean by the powerful winter surf.

■ *Left:* Cluster Cone Rocks are seen here across Bear Harbor, which is part of the Sinkyone Wilderness State Park in northern Mendocino County. This is in an area so remote and rugged it is known as California's Lost Coast. Highway engineers decided the area was so unstable and rough that they avoided it entirely, routing the main coastal road, Highway 1, many miles inland. Reached only by steep, narrow, mountain roads, the park offers excellent hiking opportunities. ■ *Above:* Periwinkle, horsetail and red alder flourish on the site of the old Bear Harbor Railroad.

■ *Above:* A large redwood stump is carried ashore by the water at the mouth of the Garcia River on Manchester State Beach in Mendocino County. The combination of vast forests, numerous rivers, and frequent winter storms assures a continuous supply of driftwood on north coast beaches, making them a beachcomber's paradise. This stump and many of the large driftwood pieces that come ashore are a result of logging along the northern coast rivers.

■ *Above:* The town of Mendocino was founded in 1852 when a shipload of San Franciscans came to the Mendocino coast and established the first successful sawmill in the area. The redwood lumber culled from the region helped build, and—after the 1906 earthquake—rebuild, San Francisco. Famous as an art community, Mendocino is viewed here from Mendocino Headlands State Park, where gardens of escaped domestic calla lilies bloom profusely.

■ *Above:* Built in 1870, the original Point Arena Lighthouse was the only brick building left standing in the town after the 1906 San Francisco Earthquake, though it was severely damaged. It was razed and rebuilt shortly thereafter, remaining a manned station until 1977 when it was fully automated. It is viewed here at sunrise from Manchester State Beach in Mendocino County. ■ *Right:* The seathrift, or *Armeria maritima,* clings to a foothold just out of the splash zone on Salt Point in Salt Point State Park in Sonoma County.

■ *Left:* The Ten Mile Dunes extend south of Ten Mile River in MacKerricher State Park. North of Fort Bragg, the 2,030-acre park contains one of California's longest continuous stretches of sandy beach and dunes. The park has many miles of hiking, bicycling and equestrian trails, along with a wooden boardwalk that leads out to a whale-watching platform. ■ *Above:* The cow parsnip is a cosmopolitan plant, growing from Alaska to the southern California mountains and from the Pacific to the Atlantic coasts. Here, it appears above Cuffy Cove, near Elk, in Mendocino County.

■ *Above:* Formed where the Gualala River meets the sea, this rich tidal estuary is prime habitat for fish and other aquatic species. Osprey, heron, duck, and a multitude of shore birds are also attracted to the wealth of available food. Gualala is pronounced "Wallala," a Spanish version of the Pomo Indian word, *Walali,* meaning "where the waters meet" or "water-coming-down place."

■ *Above:* California's heritage is distinctly Spanish, but in a few places other influences show. In 1812, a crew of Russians and Aleut Indians built a village and fort at Rossiya, only one hundred miles north of San Francisco. They came to hunt sea otter, grow food, and establish trade with the Mexican landowners. Not much came of their efforts, and little was left after the 1906 San Francisco earthquake. But the fort, now Fort Ross State Historical Park, was rebuilt and restored faithfully—and Russia lives on in Northern California.

■ *Above:* Few symbols characterize the redwood belt quite like the split-rail fence. Virgin redwood lumber, once available in great abundance, has a clear, clean grain and can be split easily to make fence posts. Redwood's hardy resistance to both rot and insects guaranteed builders a strong, long-lasting barricade for livestock. Reminders of the past, fences such as this one near the town of Mendocino are all that remain of the old homesteads.

■ *Above:* Covered with coast goldfields, the coastal bluffs in Sonoma Coast State Beach provide sharp contrast to the plunging headlands north of the Russian River. These marine terraces, so common along the coast, are old beaches that were raised above sea level by the uplift of the Coast Range and then carved to their present shape by the force and action of the waves. This gently sloping land is often used for grazing or farming.

■ *Above:* During salmon season, a parade of fishing vessels sails in and out of Bodega Bay on the Sonoma County coast. Rickety old boats and sleek, modern vessels are tied to the wharves, helping maintain the tradition of a town intimately linked with the sea.
■ *Right:* Few areas on the California coast have a concentration of seastacks like those at Shell Beach in Sonoma Coast State Beach. Formed where two tectonic plates collide along the San Andreas Fault, "Franciscan" is the geologic term that refers to the jumbled sea floor sediments forming a large portion of the Coast Range.

■ *Left and Above:* Sonoma Coast State Beach, extending thirteen miles between Bodega Head and the Russian River in Sonoma County, is a series of pocket beaches separated by rocky headlands. Each spring, dozens of species of wildflowers bloom at one time, covering the headlands with a mosaic of varying hues. Lupine and tarweed bloom together in profusion, covering every square inch of the bluffs above Shell Beach with vivid color.

■ *Above:* Mount Tamalpais State Park in Marin County offers the best views of the San Francisco Bay area—guaranteed! From Bolinas Ridge, one looks past the Golden Gate, past San Francisco, and beyond to San Pedro Point in San Mateo County, twenty miles south. ■ *Right:* The sun rises to a rare clear day on crescent-shaped Drakes Beach in Point Reyes National Seashore. Named for Sir Francis Drake, the first captain to complete his trip around the world, this beach is more often covered with fog than sunshine.

■ *Left:* Large breakers crash in Salt Point State Park while harbor seals languish undisturbed on offshore rocks. Nicknamed the "spotted" seal because their mottled coat varies in color, these are the most commonly observed of California pinnipeds. This quiet, inquisitive animal is often seen both singly and in small groups.

■ *Above:* Though no longer in use, the Point Reyes Lighthouse has a French Fresnel lens composed of more than a thousand prisms of polished glass. This station, part of Point Reyes National Seashore, is also a popular spot to watch the annual gray whale migration.

■ *Above:* North of Stinson Beach on California Highway 1, Bolinas Lagoon is a drowned valley that has developed along the San Andreas fault zone. The sinuous lines of the resulting mudflats are all that is left when the lagoon is emptied at the lowest of tides. This view from Bolinas Ridge in Mount Tamalpais State Park offers a panoramic view of the entire lagoon, along with Duxbury Point.

■ *Above:* Salmon and steelhead were once plentiful in biologically rich, pristine streams of the San Francisco Bay Area. Loss of habitat, due to environmental degradation, has reduced or eliminated these historic runs. Redwood Creek, one of the few streams that still supports these fish, drains the southwest slope of Mount Tamalpais, then flows through Muir Woods National Monument.

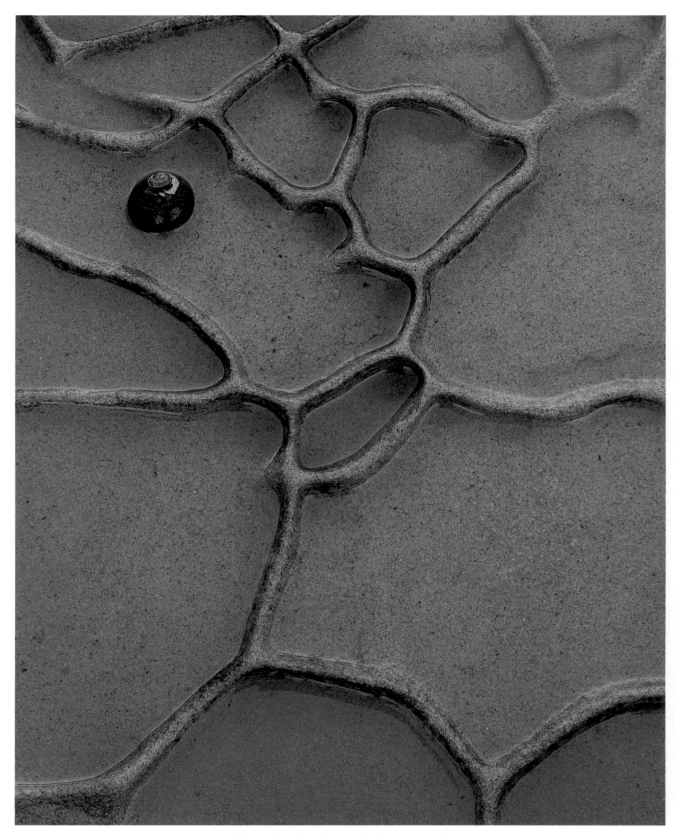

■ *Above:* Left by high tide, the shell of a sea snail rests on wave-eroded sandstone. ■ *Right:* The Golden Gate Bridge is perhaps the most identifiable landmark on the California coast. At 746 feet above water level, its two massive towers are the highest bridge towers in the world. For many, it is not only symbolic as the gateway to San Francisco, but to all of California. This view of the bridge is from Fort Baker Military Reservation in Marin County.

Big Sur Magic And Wildlife Drama

For every two days a convict spent building the road, he got three days taken off his prison sentence. None seemed to mind that his net income was seventy-five cents a day or that his living quarters were makeshift camps. The pluses were enormous: reduced time, no prison uniforms, and no gun-carrying guards. Besides, the scenery along the portion of the California coast that was known as Big Sur was some of the most spectacular any of them had ever seen.

Beginning in 1920, road construction continued for seventeen years, due to erratic funding, engineering problems, and unpredictable weather. It was a monumental task: five huge shovels moved fifteen hundred cubic yards of dirt daily; more than ten million cubic yards of rock were blasted away; one power shovel ended up in the ocean; several lives were lost; and one prisoner escaped. In the end, the road between Carmel and San Simeon traversed ninety-three miles that crawled up the face of scarps, twisted around promontories, scooted along the shoreline, wound into canyons, and crossed no less than thirty-two streams. Even the bridges were notable: seventeen of redwood trestles, seven of concrete, and eight of steel. Prize among them was the bridge at Bixby Creek, a 550-foot-high, 260-foot-long engineering masterpiece which, in its day, was the largest single-arch concrete span in the world.

By the time the road was extended to San Luis Obispo on the south and Monterey on the north, the 136-mile stretch of highway was $8.5 million over budget, bringing the total cost to nearly $10 million—an average of seventy-one thousand Depression dollars per mile. But what wonderful miles they were. And still are. Today it is part of State Highway 1, though when it opened in June of 1937 it was officially called the Great Roosevelt Highway. By 1950 it was renamed the Cabrillo Highway, and in 1966 Lady Bird Johnson and California Governor Pat Brown proclaimed it the nation's first Scenic Highway.

But whatever the title, one fact is obvious: the narrow road hairpins along one of the most celebrated stretches of coastline in the world. The Spanish priests at the Carmel Mission originally named the area *El Pais Grande del Sur*, "the big country of the south." It was a land where the massive shoulders of the Santa Lucia Mountains rose straight up out of the sea to heights of more than three thousand feet and offshore rocks waited to carve the bottom out of passing ships; where sea lions argued over squatter's rights to sun-washed rock piles and sea otters slept on kelpy waterbeds; where the threatening surf pummeled cobbles into sand and the emerald forests plunged toward the sea through steep-cut ravines.

The terrain was such a geographic nightmare that under both Spain's and Mexico's control it remained largely unsettled by the white man. Easy to see why: bulging headlands, jagged rocks, perpendicular cliffs, and no safe harbor from San Simeon to Monterey. If that were not bad enough, the Santa Lucias were a double—and in places a triple—mountain range that rose to heights of nearly six thousand feet and stretched all the way from the edge of Carmel Valley south to Point San Luis. It was a 120-mile-long, 35-mile-wide swath of sedimentary bluffs, granitic headwalls, and ancient marine terraces with such formidable presence that even the most cursory exploration seemed too great an undertaking.

And then the Americans came. By 1846, with California now a United States possession, the "big country of the south" was open for preemption—a law stating that anyone could settle on 160 acres of public land provided he kept the land in good condition and planted at least one crop. The purchase price was $1.25 an acre and was due within a year. By 1862, a new law was on the books—the Homestead Act, much the same as the Preemption Act with one laudable exception: the land was free.

By 1872 the first Big Sur homesteaders had built themselves a short wagon road in the northern section, and by the 1880s they had extended it all the way to the southern end of Big Sur Valley. By the turn of the century the tourists began to arrive via horse and stagecoach, and by 1918 the move was on to get a proper highway built. Once the asphalt was in place, the trip from Monterey to Big Sur no longer took the better part of a day, and with the new ease of entry, realtors and investment companies began their advertising pitch: "Sunshine, scenery, views, water, all in thirty minutes' time from Monterey. Cabin sites as low as a

Left: *The profile of a seastack at Martin's Beach, San Mateo County, as it was altered by the Loma Prieta earthquake of October 17, 1989*

hundred dollars; acreage from twenty-five dollars up . . . on the highway with a magnificent view."

The view is still magnificent; the terrain, still exceedingly rugged; the land, still sparsely settled. Change any single characteristic and you lose the magic that is Big Sur. To all intents, the spell takes hold just beyond Morro Bay and grows ever more intense as the road twists northward: past Piedras Blancas Point where a guano-covered rock rises up out of the sea like a ghostly leviathan of eons-past; along the ridge of Ragged Point and its heart-thumping drop into the ocean; past Jade Cove, Sand Dollar Beach, and Limekiln Beach Redwoods Campground, site of one of the nation's steepest coastal canyons.

On and on the road unwinds, each curve revealing views more mesmerizing than the last, and when at last you find yourself at the heart of Big Sur Valley, the realization dawns that a spell has been cast and you have succumbed. Words may never suffice to explain Big Sur's intangible qualities: there are many places where the land meets the sea; a galaxy of wildflowers bedazzles the eye; redwoods grace shadowy canyons; deer browse the brush; and coyotes sing long into the night. But they are not Big Sur. And understanding the difference means having known the magic.

Tantalizing as the scenery between Morro Bay and Carmel is, there is yet another reason for the area's noteworthiness. Here, where the kelp forests are so dense they appear as gigantic bronze bruises on the sea, lives a host of resilient little animals whose fur is the most luxuriant in the world. Scientifically, it is *Enhydra lutris*. More commonly, the sea otter.

Today approximately seventeen hundred of these playful little creatures live along the central California coast—sixteen hundred more than there were fifty years ago; sixteen thousand fewer than before the Russians and Aleuts up at Fort Ross began their methodical process of sea otter hunting.

A cousin of the mink, the sea otter spends its life close to shore, living in groups called rafts. Generally males live with males, and females with females and pups—though sometimes a contrary otter chooses to live alone. Pups are born at sea in winter, and though their mothers nurse them for several months, the pups soon become proficient at grabbing bits of clam or mussel or abalone or squid or—most prized of all—purple sea urchin off mom's chest and chomping it down with all thirty-two of its newborn teeth.

Because sea otters have no thick, insulating layer of protective fat as do other sea mammals, the otter spends much of its day grooming its fur by blowing air into the spaces between its eight hundred million hairs. If as little as a quarter of its fur becomes soiled, the otter's normal body temperature of 100° Fahrenheit drops and the animal freezes to death. Moms not only have to keep their own fur in tip-top shape, but their pup's too. Because baby-tending is a full-time job, an otter mother is able to care for only one, and if, by chance, twins are born, one will be abandoned and most likely die. Unless, of course, it is found by one of the several agencies involved in sea otter rescue and rehabilitation—of which one of the foremost is the Monterey Bay Aquarium.

International legislation passed in 1911 protecting the sea otter appeared to be a day late and a dollar short, as for the most part the gregarious little animal was considered extinct. Then, in 1938, the extraordinary happened. A small colony of sea otters was found living in the kelp beds offshore of Bixby Creek on the Big Sur coast. The secret was well-kept for many years, and, in the meantime, the clowns of the kelp grew in number. Today, though their population is far from equaling the original, the California sea otter is highly visible—floating on its back, diving for food, somersaulting in the kelp, and sleeping with its hands and feet above water—as though it had just come from the manicurist and was waiting for its nails to dry.

The kelp beds that are both home and life to the sea otter are mostly comprised of a brown algae known as *Macrocystis pyrifera*, or giant kelp. It is the biggest aquatic plant in the world and one of the fastest growers, pushing itself upward as much as a foot a day under water and two feet a day along the surface. Anchored to a rocky sea floor by an immense tangle of pencil-thin holdfasts, the giant kelp's stalk and numerous leaflike blades are all held in an upright position by a plethora of gas-filled floats. Nourishment comes from the seawater itself and must be rich in growth-boosting nutrients, for the giant kelp often reaches heights of two hundred feet.

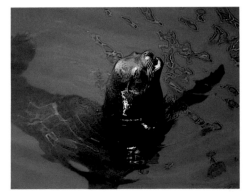

This swaying forest of the sea is one of the most prolific habitats on earth. More than thirty species of fish, eighty species of algae, and at least three hundred kinds of microinvertebrates such as sea stars and abalone thrive here. In all, the kelp forest supports three times more fish than ocean terrain without kelp, and such abundance draws all manner of marine creatures into the forest folds—each one hoping to eat without being eaten.

Oddly enough, the greatest threat to the forest is a prickly little animal, the sea urchin. Although all sea urchins are dangerous to the kelp, the purple variety is the worst. The problem is its humongous appetite. Unchecked, the purple urchin can reproduce so quickly that a square yard may contain more than three hundred of them, and in such numbers, it can destroy whole kelp beds with chainsawlike proficiency.

Fortunately, the purple urchin is the sea otters' favorite food. So many are eaten, in fact, that the sea otters' teeth and bones eventually take on a purple tint. Yet problems still exist for this underwater forest. For although the sea otters' current range extends about 220 miles between Point Año Nuevo and Point San Luis, the kelp beds grow all along the Pacific Coast of North America—the otters' original habitat. With few natural predators to control the urchins now, the plants, called the "sequoias of the sea" by Jacques Cousteau, could one day find themselves headed for the rare and endangered list.

Although monarch butterflies are neither rare nor endangered, the insects' annual migration is so uncommon in the insect world that the United States Government has declared it an endangered phenomenon. To scientists, the monarch is *Danaus plexippus;* to the rest of us, it is simply the large orange and black butterfly with white polka dots on its wing edges. Originally a member of the tropics, the monarch long ago migrated into temperate zones. Today, it is primarily an insect of the Western Hemisphere, and although its velvety wings grace nearly every part of its adopted territory, when the cold season is at hand the monarchs all follow the same instinct: to migrate south.

They are the only insect known to do so. Most of the one hundred million North American monarchs that summer east of the Rocky Mountains head for Mexico, Florida, and Guatemala. The five million or so monarchs west of the Rockies—including those from southwestern Canada—migrate to the central California coast, with a few traveling as far south as Baja California. Migratory flights have been documented through tagging, with the award for the longest-known flight going to a monarch tagged near Toronto, Canada, and captured in Mexico—a trip of 1,870 miles, not counting all the zig-zag miles added during the insect's normal daily activity.

There are about one hundred major overwintering grounds on the West Coast, and the largest—not only in California but throughout the entire United States—is at Natural Bridges State Beach in Santa Cruz. The eucalyptus grove here is rather nondescript; the park, often filled with people. But still the monarchs come—between fifty thousand and two hundred thousand each year. On sunny days they spread out in search of fresh water and flower nectar. At night or during cool days, they cling to tree branches by the hundreds of thousands, giving the effect of a tree in full bloom of brilliant orange.

Perhaps the most amazing phenomenon is not that the insects migrate or that they frequent the same groves year after year, but that not one of the butterflies has ever been there before. Neither were its parents. Or its grandparents. The overwintering monarchs are five to six generations removed from those that graced the trees last year, and though each migrates individually, all somehow end up in the same places. So far, science has no explanation in light of one fact: none lives long enough to make the round trip. Spring- or summer-hatched monarchs live only about six weeks; autumn- or winter-hatched monarchs have a lifespan of about six months.

Each begins life far from the overwintering grounds. As the females follow the spring growing season north, they lay their eggs on the undersides of milkweed plants, and in three to five days wormlike larvae hatch. In approximately two weeks the greedy little worm outgrows and sheds its skin five times to become a caterpillar twenty-seven hundred times as large as when it hatched. Usually the fifth molting results in the chrysalis stage in which the caterpillar metamorphoses, or changes its form. Within two weeks the jade chrysalis splits, and a damp, limp monarch butterfly emerges. In just a few days the females

begin to lay eggs, and their progeny, like their forebears, will live about six weeks.

By late August or early September, autumn monarchs begin to store fat in readiness of migration. Staying too long in areas that freeze means certain death, for these butterflies must maintain a body temperature of between forty and one hundred degrees. So by the hundreds of thousands they head south—flashes of orange gracing the sky, held aloft by wings as soft as flower petals and nearly as fragile.

Not all survive the entire trip, for even though natural predators are few, they do exist. Yet on and on they travel, flying at twenty to thirty miles per hour; cruising at fifteen miles per hour; gliding at less than fourteen miles per hour. Somehow, the majority reach their overwintering grounds and settle in. The "wanderer" is back—to a place it has never been.

Wildlife drama along the central coast is perpetual. Within this endless variation of sand and sea, flocks of spindly-legged sanderlings dance along the ocean's edge, following each advancing and receding wave in some sort of avian choreography; brown pelicans fly above the surf, performing aerial maneuvers that would put the Blue Angels to shame; harbor seals openly spy on human beachwalkers, following them back and forth for no other reason than natural curiosity. In winter, the gray whales glide by, headed for their Baja California birthing and breeding grounds, and in spring they come again—babes in tow—headed back toward their Arctic homes.

In December the male northern elephant seals haul out their enormous bulk onto Año Nuevo Island just north of Santa Cruz and begin their noisy, bloody battles for dominance. Inflating their huge snouts they snort and bellow at one another, creating a clamor so intense it resonates for at least a mile. When visual and vocal threats fail to dissuade some hopeful bachelor, canine teeth come into play with such vengeance that there are few, if any, adult male elephant seals that are not excessively scarred.

By the time the battles are over, in late December, the pregnant females arrive to join the dominant bulls' harems. Pups are born about a week later, woolly-looking babies that tip the scales at around seventy pounds. But this is miniscule compared to their parents: females weigh twelve to eighteen hundred pounds; males, over two tons. But baby grows fast on mom's milk, the richest of all milk, with a 55 percent fat content. Within a month the pup weighs as much as four hundred pounds, and usually by the time it is six weeks old it has been abandoned—for mom has mated once again and headed out to sea.

The world's largest mainland population of northern elephant seals resides at Año Nuevo State Reserve where the assemblage of four thousand individuals is strung out between the offshore island and the mainland beach. Hunted nearly into extinction in the 1800s by the whaling industry, which wanted the animals' oil-rich blubber, the northern elephant seal has made a monumental comeback. By 1892, there were fewer than fifty left in the world, all living on Guadalupe Island off the coast of Baja. Mexico declared them a protected species, and by 1930 the United States Government had followed its lead.

Little by little, the elephant seals grew in number and returned to their old haunts. The vanguard arrived at Año Nuevo in 1955, and five years later the first pup was born. By 1978 pup births at Año Nuevo numbered 872, and by 1975 the population had grown so large the thirteen-acre island was no longer big enough to accommodate the elephant seals as well as the many sea lions and harbor seals who had also taken up residence. With quarters so blubber-packed, the elephant seal females had no choice other than to give birth on the mainland beach amidst a crowd of bachelor males and juveniles with nothing better to do than fight over presumed territories.

Along the central coast, it is said nature has driven a hard bargain for its beauty. Maybe so. The region's myriad sea stacks and offshore isles have been hewn from the mainland by rock-pulverizing waves that left shattered testimonies of land's former edge.

Miles of sand dunes are evidence of erosion of the Coast Range, for bit by bit the ocean's roaring waters have chewed up the mountains, washed them out to sea, then piled them back on shore one grain at a time. Centuries of weathering have uncovered the volcanic plug called Morro Rock, and eons of wave-powered uppercuts have set apart the rocky fist known as Point Sur. The assault on the terrain has been horrendous. Anything else would have been from too common a mold.

Right: *The Hyde Street Pier on San Francisco's Fisherman's Wharf, where real working boats dock and go fishing every day*

■ *Left:* The Columbus Tower, built in 1905, was one of the few buildings in North Beach to survive the 1906 San Francisco earthquake. Its architecture contrasts strikingly with the Transamerica Pyramid, built in 1972. ■ *Above:* The San Francisco-Oakland Bay Bridge links San Francisco with the East Bay cities and is the world's longest suspension span. From Yerba Buena Island, the winter sunset is directly over San Francisco's downtown skyline.

■ *Above:* Pigeon Point is the second tallest lighthouse in the United States, measuring 115 feet. The former Coast Guard Station, built in 1872, is now operated as a hostel for travelers on the San Mateo County coast. ■ *Right:* Several species of gulls migrate from cooler northern climates to spend the winter on the California coast. Each autumn, huge flocks congregate at the mouth of Pescadero Creek at Pescadero State Beach in San Mateo County.

■ *Left:* The thick bark of the coast redwood is impregnated with tannin, the substance that protects the trees from disease and fire and helps them achieve their famous longevity. Further protection came to this grove in the Santa Cruz Mountains in 1902, when a successful campaign preserved these trees within the Big Basin Redwoods State Park. The creation of this first state park was the beginning of the California State Park System. ■ *Above:* An eroded sandstone arch marks the south end of Four Mile Beach in Wilder Ranch State Park, an undeveloped park in Santa Cruz County.

■ *Above:* The Santa Cruz Boardwalk's long history began in 1868 when bathhouses were built along the sandy beach. The next stage of evolution came in 1907 when the Casino Building, with its large, ornate arches, was completed. Then the boardwalk began in earnest its current role as an amusement park. The 1911 Looff Carousel and the 1924 Giant Dipper, both Historic Landmarks, have continued to thrill succeeding generations of boardwalkers.

■ *Above:* California's coast was once generously sprinkled with seaside fun parks, offering boardwalks to stroll, sandy beaches to swim and summertime play. The Boardwalk at Santa Cruz is one of the few survivors. ■ *Overleaf:* Monterey, for many of the years between 1775 and 1846 the provincial capital of Alta California, was and still is a beautiful city. The many historic buildings are well preserved and provide the history buff with a toe hold on the past.

■ *Above:* Built in 1827, the Custom House in Monterey State Historical Park is the oldest government building in the state of California. It served as Mexico's provincial capital during a long period of prosperity that ended when the United States took possession of the territory. On July 7, 1846, Commodore John Drake Sloat raised the flag of the United States of America for the first time in the area, claiming six hundred thousand square miles.

■ *Above:* The Monterey Bay Aquarium is not a place; it is an experience. Since its opening in 1984, almost two million people have gone through the glass doors each year to see the wonders of Monterey Bay without getting wet. On the site of the old Hovden Cannery, the aquarium is a memorial to the history of Cannery Row and a celebration of the rich marine life of the Monterey Bay. The Kelp Forest is the tallest aquarium exhibit in the world.

■ *Above:* John Steinbeck, author of such classics as *The Grapes of Wrath* and *Cannery Row,* is Salinas' most famous native son. His writings focused international attention on Salinas Valley and the Monterey Bay area, bringing familiarity and appreciation to the country he knew and loved. The house he was born and raised in has been preserved and is listed in the Registry of Historic Places.

■ *Above:* The Mision San Carlos Borromeo del Rio Carmelo, now called the Carmel Mission, was Father Serra's residence and head-quarters until his death in 1784. It was from here that he directed both the founding and the affairs of seven other missions along the coast of California. The well-kept gardens and magnificent church are highlights of this, the second built of California's missions.

■ *Above:* Scenic Coast Highway 1 through Big Sur, completed in 1937, heads toward Bixby Creek Bridge. This winding, narrow road clings to one of California's most dramatic coastlines, running through haunting, rugged terrain long considered to be a haven for writers, painters, and artists. ■ *Right:* A cypress snag, with twisted trunk and battered limbs, hugs the cliff above Headland Cove in Point Lobos State Reserve. Its bleached, gray form is evidence of hardships endured, but even in death the beauty of this celebrated symbol of the Monterey coast is still unmistakable.

■ *Left:* Countless years of wave action have polished these granite boulders in Abalone Cove in Garrapata State Park. ■ *Above:* The sea continually shapes and reshapes the coastline, creating a saw-toothed shore where the wind-whipped waves chew up the rocky headlands, pummel boulders into cobbles, and sculpt free-form arches that eventually collapse—leaving tiny islets as ghostly reminders of the land's former edge. This arch is at Pfeiffer Beach in Los Padres National Forest along the Big Sur coast.

■ *Above:* Viewed here from Highway 1, the massive headland at Point Sur rises more than three hundred feet above the surf. The Point Sur Lighthouse, perched on the rocky flank, guides ships' captains with its reliable beacon in much the same way as it has since it was first put into service in 1889. This section of the Big Sur coast is protected in the California Sea Otter State Game Refuge, and the playful mammals are often seen in the kelp beds offshore.

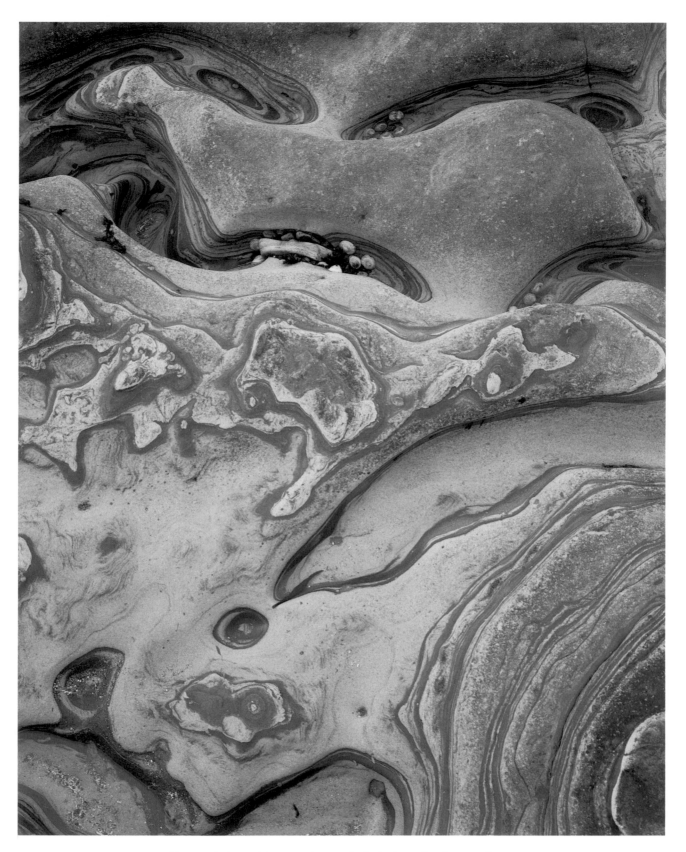

■ *Above:* A low tide reveals eroded designs in the sandstone at Weston Beach in Point Lobos State Reserve. First created in 1933, the nation's first underwater preserve was established here when 750 submerged acres were added to the state reserve in 1960. Divers now get in line early each weekend to have a chance to explore the rich and diverse kelp forests of this watery Reserve.

■ *Above:* As the Big Sur River leaves the 159,000-acre Ventana Wilderness, it enters the Big Sur River Gorge in Pfeiffer Big Sur State Park. A short walk from the campground, the gorge includes groves of redwoods, big leaf maples, and deep river pools. ■ *Right:* As a Pacific winter storm rages, the surf pounds the granite-cobbled beach at Soberanes Creek in Garrapata State Park.

■ *Left:* Pampas-grass-covered hillsides meet the sea on the Big Sur coast near the hamlet of Lucia. ■ *Above:* In the distance, Morro Rock and Point Buchon are barely visible from Highway 46 in the Santa Lucia Range. ■ *Overleaf:* Of California's seventeen National Forests, only the Los Padres borders the Pacific Ocean. Within it are some of the most dramatic vistas on the entire coast. One example is a view of Twin Peak and Lopez Point from Pacific Valley.

■ *Above:* Beyond the influence of the coastal fog belt, valley oaks flourish on the rolling hills of the Coast Range in San Luis Obispo County. ■ *Right:* At sunrise, sand dunes in Morro Bay State Park are a striking foreground to the distant peaks of the Santa Lucia Range. Morro Bay is one of our coast's best preserved estuarian habitats. During low tides, nearly fourteen hundred acres of mudflats are exposed, attracting more than 250 species of birds.

■ *Left:* Rising 581 feet at the entrance to Morro Bay, Morro Rock dominates the landscape for miles. This volcanic plug is a nesting site for the endangered peregrine falcon. Once near extinction, these birds are making a healthy comeback, thanks to a captive breeding program and the banning of DDT. ■ *Above:* Formed by volcanic activity more than twenty million years ago, Bishop Peak is one of six conical peaks that puncture the sky between Morro Bay and San Luis Obispo. Morro Rock is the westernmost and best-known of these volcanic plugs, but all are visible from Highway 1.

■ *Above:* The Pismo Beach Pier juts out into the Pacific at Pismo State Beach. This strand is the most popular clam-digging area on the California coast. ■ *Right:* In February, the coast paintbrush, *Castilleja affinis,* blooms in the Guadalupe Dunes section of the Nature Conservancy's Nipomo Dunes Preserve in San Luis Obispo County. ■ *Overleaf:* A winter sunrise brushes Guadalupe Dunes in the Nature Conservancy's Nipomo Dunes Preserve. The Nature Conservancy, an international conservation organization, manages over thirty-five hundred acres in the Nipomo Dunes.

■ *Left:* At low tide, green and blue-green algae are exposed in the impressive tidepool area below Margo Dodd City Park at Shell Beach in San Luis Obispo County. ■ *Above:* The spectacular blooms of giant coreopsis appear each spring on the headlands above Destroyer Rock on Vandenberg Air Force Base. Much of the base's nearly one hundred thousand acres is managed by the U.S. Air Force to protect biological diversity. ■ *Overleaf:* Elmer Ross, accessible only via a spiral staircase, is a quiet pocket beach tucked away from other major beaches in the Pismo area.

■ *Above:* The moon sets over Nipomo Dunes near Oso Flaco Lake in the Pismo Dunes State Vehicular Recreation Area in San Luis Obispo County. ■ *Right:* A moderate marine climate and rich soil combine to make California's shoreline acres perfect for farming. Though much productive land is being lost to urbanization and the acceleration of land prices, the agricultural industry is still booming. Artichokes, well adapted to a temperate climate, are one of the more famous crops. This farm, nestled against the Casmalia Hills on the Point Sal Road, is one of many along the coast.

Sun Fun And Island Wilds

On a clear day you can see the far-distant Coronado Islands, their rounded domes rising out of the Baja (Lower) California waters like the tops of gigantic heads. More than four hundred feet straight down on the right is the ever-restless Pacific Ocean; in front, the broad channel of San Diego Bay backed by the amber beaches of North Island and the Silver Strand; to the left, the fifteen-mile-long curved finger of San Diego Bay itself. Such is the scene from the tip of Point Loma, home of Cabrillo National Monument—a place where the view is said to be one of the best in the world and the monument is rated as the second most heavily visited federal park in the United States.

Most visitors come for the view. Or, in winter, to watch the gray whale migration. Others come to investigate the old Point Loma Lighthouse, one of the original eight West Coast lighthouses. A few come out of curiosity, for if truth were told, the name Juan Rodriguez Cabrillo has never lain close to the tip of history's tongue—so why is there a national monument named after him?

Easy to understand once you know the facts. Just fifty years after Columbus discovered America, Cabrillo sailed up from Mexico in command of two Spanish exploring vessels and entered waters that had never before felt the wake of any craft bigger than an Indian canoe. It was a journey of incredible dimensions, especially considering that the two stubby ships were each less than one hundred feet long, with crew quarters greatly open to the weather, and the prevailing winds hard against them.

It was Juan Rodriguez who claimed the honor of being the first European to enter San Diego Bay. It was, he noted, "a landlocked and very good harbor . . . which was very long." Six days later, after waiting out a "very great gale" in a port so "good they felt nothing," Cabrillo once again set his sails north. And though historians disagree on exactly how far he got, all agree that Juan Rodriguez Cabrillo was the first white man to set foot on the Alta (Upper) California coast.

Had it not been for legends, myths, rumors, truths, and half-truths, Cabrillo and his predecessors might never have discovered and settled the southern California coast at all, and the influence in the state as a whole would likely be something other than Spanish. But fate was at work. Early in the 1500s, a book called *Sergas de Esplandián* by Ordonez de Montalvo became popular in Spain, and, though it was actually a work of fiction, parts of it began to take hold of the people. In no time at all, the Spaniards were considering whether Montalvo was telling more truth than fiction when he wrote "at the right hand of the Indies there is an island named California, very close to that part of the Terrestrial Paradise." A legend was in the making.

Myth began to suggest that the island was not only real, but was inhabited solely by women whose weapons were fashioned of gold and precious stones and that these women were protected by many griffins—creatures which were half-lion and half-man—creatures that could be found nowhere else on earth. Myth also whispered that this island was ruled by Queen Calafia, a woman of majestic proportions, very beautiful and in the vigor of her womanhood, with a heart that was brave, and ambitions that were noble.

Rumor stated that somewhere along this uncharted coast lay the strait of Anian, which was thought to be a shortcut connecting the Atlantic and the Pacific oceans and through which European traders could more easily access the wealth of the Spice Islands. And so it was that the explorers came. And so it was that they discovered coastal California. Then, believing it to be an island—perhaps the very island mentioned in Montalvo's book—they named it California.

Years later truth reared its head and stated that although Spain claimed California by right of discovery, the territory remained unsettled and as such was up for grabs. Half-truth gossiped that the Russians were coming—long before they actually did—and had it not been for that particular half-truth, King Charles of Spain might never have issued his panicked decree that Alta California should be settled immediately.

And so it was. On July 1, 1769, the Spanish flag was raised atop a small hill that overlooked the San Diego River and stood within two musket shots of the bay. The settlement was called San Diego de Alcala, and in the beginning, it consisted of a mission and a presidio. In

Left: *The sandstone headlands of Gaviota State Park, part of the oil-bearing Monterey formation*

charge of spiritual matters was Father Junipero Serra, President Superior of the California missions; in charge of law and order was Gaspar de Portola, commander-in-chief of the crack Spanish dragoons. Settlement of Alta California had begun—two hundred and twenty-seven years after Cabrillo had first claimed the land for the Spanish crown.

In the more than two hundred years since the initial settlement, much along the south coast has changed. Gone are most of the freshwater marshes and the tidal flats. Rivers have been diked and diverted, and most of those remaining have been channeled into concrete ditches. Neon pierces the nighttime sky, giving it an almost ethereal incandescence.

People and automobiles are everywhere, and, despite a laid-back lifestyle, the pace is oftentimes hectic. Of all the California coast, it is in the south that civilization has most crowded in.

Those who live there love it. So what if people are packed like sardines along the wide, sandy beaches? Only on the south coast can you boast a year-round tan. And who cares if traffic moves with glacial slowness? Everything you could possibly want is only a short distance away. And what's the big deal about a hectic pace? Getting your work done quickly means more time in the sun. Or on the tennis court. Or in a sailboat. Or on the golf course. Cabrillo should have had it so good; Portola could have wished for nothing better.

Somehow, pockets of wilderness have survived the onslaught of mankind, and most are today held in trust by county, state, or federal agencies. They are places that grip our attention if for no other reason than the fact that their pristine beauty stands out from their surroundings as distinctly as a bride in a room full of three-piece suits.

These ecological islands are few; their regions limited. Even so, they are places where motley mobs of shorebirds and seabirds hold raucous gatherings, and wind-scrolled sand gives the beach the appearance of having been overlain with corrugated cardboard; where some of the world's rarest pine trees cling to the tops of sandstone bluffs and children can still follow a trail through brown, raspy grass and discover for themselves the south coast of centuries past.

If there is any single area where everything that is still wild in southern California comes together, it is in the Channel Islands. Strung out along the coast like the beads of a necklace, the eight islands are called Anacapa, Santa Cruz, Santa Rosa, San Miguel, Santa Barbara, San Nicholas, Santa Catalina, and San Clemente. They begin south of Point Conception and end north of San Diego. Among the first parts of the California coast to be explored by Cabrillo and his party, the Channel Islands are today still much as they were, and among their many intrigues is the fact that an incredible amount of their flora and fauna is endemic—species that have evolved in the islands' relative isolation and are found nowhere else on earth.

In some instances, island animals retain characteristics similar to their counterparts on the mainland, though their many years of sequestered living have resulted in size, shape, or color variations.

All the islands except Anacapa and Santa Barbara, the two smallest, boast their own version of the island fox, a housecat-sized relative of the mainland gray fox. And though all eight islands house their own larger renditions of the mainland deer mouse, only Santa Rosa and Santa Cruz have the island interpretation of the spotted skunk, and only Santa Cruz itself claims the island scrub jay—a brassy bird equally as sassy as its mainland kinsmen though a good 25 percent larger.

Scientists believe that the four northern islands of Anacapa, Santa Cruz, Santa Rosa, and San Miguel were once connected—a sort of super island covering 724 square miles. During the last Ice Age, around eighteen thousand years ago, this island, which the scientists call Santarosae, lay much closer to shore. The sea level was lower then, and the Santa Barbara Channel was supposedly fewer than four miles at its narrowest. Just right for swimming across. Not surprisingly, some creatures must have done just that. But none more intriguing than the mammoths.

Once on Santarosae, the lumbering behemoths settled in. Then, as the Ice Age came to a close, the melting ice slowly began to raise the level of the sea. Santarosae gradually became separated into four individual islands; the channel stretched to thirteen miles at its narrowest point. The mammoths, now stranded, eventually evolved

into paradoxical pygmy mammoths—creatures only four to six feet high at the shoulder. Exactly how long they plodded around their much-shrunken domain is anyone's guess, but the fact is that fossil bones of both the imperial and pygmy mammoths have been discovered on several of the islands—in one instance, right next to the firepit of prehistoric Indians.

Barbequed mammoth for lunch? No one knows for sure whether the bones happened to be there by chance or design. For that matter, no one knows for sure exactly how long prehistoric man lived there, though radiocarbon dating reveals that it was at least eight to nine thousand years ago. In historic times, especially during Cabrillo's voyage, the islands were filled with Indian villages—Chumash on the northern islands and Gabrielino on the southern islands.

The Spaniards recorded their first meetings with the Indians in their journals, writing down lengthy observations. ". . . Here came canoes with fish to barter; the Indians were very friendly . . . all the way there were many canoes, for the whole coast is very densely populated. . . ."

They described the dress and adornment of the women, noting that from the waist down they wore very soft buckskin that had been fringed along the edges and ornamented with beads or shells. From the waist up their dress was a modest cape of either rabbit, otter, squirrel, or fox. They wore necklaces and earrings. Their hairstyle consisted of short bangs combed forward and singed daily with a piece of pinebark in order that not one hair should protrude. The rest of their hair was worn loose and slicked down on top—and nearly all sported sidelocks. Their total appearance, said the early journalists, was one of neatness and grace.

Some diarists noted that the men went totally naked; others related that the Indian men covered themselves to some small degree with a waist-length cloak fashioned of rabbit, fox, sea otter, or hare—though the chiefs were allowed to wear a cloak that reached to their ankles. Around the waist, the men wore a sort of belt in which they carried knives and other objects, and their hair, though very long, was tied up with strings that had been interwoven into the hair, and the whole coiffure ornamented with decorations made of bone or wood.

For the most part, the journals all agreed that the Indian men were well built and friendly as well as alert, agile, and ingenious. Nearly all had the thick part of their nose pierced, and all had their ears perforated with two large holes from which dangled canelike earrings filled with the powder of wild tobacco.

Fashions and facial adornments aside, the Indians of the islands were an inventive and adaptable people who made bows of elderberry wood and fishhooks out of deer bones; baby powder of wild rose petals and flu remedies out of sage leaves; dishes from abalone shells and chewing gum out of milkweed sap; sandpaper from sharkskin and glue from pine tree pitch.

The Chumash were especially noted for their shellbead money, which they made by drilling holes in olivella shells with seal or sea lion whiskers and then stringing them on hemp stems. Denominations were measured by wrapping the shellbead string around the hand, with each wrap equalling a set amount. Because the Chumash supplied almost all the shellbead money used by the southern California Indians in their extensive trade network, they became one of the wealthiest tribes in the state's southern section.

By the mid-1800s, most of the island Chumash had left to join their mainland relatives in coastal missions, and today there is little evidence of their passing. For the most part, the islands are now either federally or privately owned. In 1938, President Franklin D. Roosevelt declared Santa Barbara and Anacapa as Channel Islands National Monument, and a year later, he extended the monument boundary to include the surrounding waters.

In 1980, Congress designated the islands of Anacapa, Santa Cruz, Santa Rosa, San Miguel, and Santa Barbara as well as 125,000 acres of submerged lands as the Channel Islands National Park; later that same year, the Channel Islands Marine Sanctuary was founded, an area extending six nautical miles around each island in the park. It is administered by the National Oceanic and Atmospheric Administration and managed by the park in cooperation with the California Department of Fish and Game.

In a section of the state so densely populated, the Channel Islands are the last stronghold for breeding seals and sea lions. Six species breed on the islands' sandy

beaches, rocky slopes, and offshore rocks. Hands-down winner for hosting the largest pinniped convention on the south coast is San Miguel. The favorite hauling-out site is Point Bennett, a sprawling peninsula that, at any given time, is jammed with tons of the bellowing blubber known as California sea lions, northern elephant seals, harbor seals, northern fur seals, and—many times—steller sea lions and Guadalupe fur seals.

While the lowlands play host to the pinnipeds, the islands' pockmarked cliffs and terraced flats are home to thousands of marine and land birds. As a whole, the Channel Islands constitute the most important nesting area south of the Farallons and one of the major breeding areas in the entire northeastern Pacific. Once again, San Miguel plays prime host, housing at least 60 percent of all the birds nesting on the Channel Islands. Here are more than ten thousand pairs of Cassin's auklets, plump little birds often called seal quail, and all around them, like a beehive of birds, are hundreds of cormorants, storm petrels, pigeon guillemots, black oyster catchers, western gulls, and Xantus' murrelets.

Taking second place as bird host is Santa Barbara Island, a rookery of major proportions in its own right. Here is the largest nesting population of Xantus' murrelets in the entire United States—and maybe the world. Each spring, thousands of these expert divers and rapid underwater swimmers arrive on the island to nest in burrows along the steep hillsides and cliff faces. By the time the hatchlings are but forty-eight hours old they purposely tumble out of the nest and down into the sea to join their parents in swimming out into the ocean. They spend their entire lives in the watery realm and return to land only to nest.

There is more to these primitive pockets of islandic beauty than can be told. Anacapa claims some of the best tidepools left on the south coast, and Santa Rosa boasts a small grove of the rare Torrey pine. (A more extensive stand is in Del Mar, north of San Diego.) Santa Catalina, Santa Cruz, Santa Rosa, and San Clemente are all home to the relict ironwood tree, and Anacapa hosts the only permanent colony of nesting brown pelicans on the West Coast of the United States.

Nearly all the islands are pocked by archeological sites that are millenniums-old and San Miguel, Santa Rosa, San Nicholas, and San Clemente all have extensive deposits of caliche—fossil forests created ages ago as windblown lime and sand mixed together to form a natural cement that eventually encased many living plants and trees. In time, the trapped flora decomposed, leaving behind a sort of plaster casting of its former self.

If there is any one entity that denotes the south coast mainland, it is its beaches. They stretch south from Point Conception like a wide belt separating the land from the sea. At any given time of year, sun worshipers sprout like weeds along the untold miles of golden sand. The beaches are beautiful, and they are popular. Residents and visitors alike use them for walking along. Or for exercising—themselves, the dog, or both. They use them for daydreaming, or just for squeezing toes in the soft, warm sand and gathering the empty houses of long-gone mollusks or peering into tiny pools of squirming life.

Sometimes the beaches are used for listening—to the continual roar of wind and waves clashing against one another or the soft mewing of seagulls sky-hopping the air currents. Oftentimes the beaches are used for nothing more than looking—at sand dunes anchored against the sea and held fast by beach grasses, or saltbush standing defiantly against the decimating salty spray. Other times the beaches are places used in a way that is far more spiritual than worldly—for it is here that one sees with the eyes and understands with the heart the meaning of strength amidst calm and the far-reaching vastness that must surely embody eternity.

In truth, Southern Californians wear their land like a prized cloak. It is something treasured, albeit greatly used. In this place where foggy days are rare and ocean waters are far more tropical than farther north, life along the ocean edge is perpetual. Little wonder. The land here has a soft, inviting texture that mesmerizes the soul. It has been said by those along the north and central coast that they have all the brawn and the beauty. But south coast aficionados are quick to answer that they have all the fun and the sun. Who knows? Maybe Ordonez de Montalvo *was* telling more truth than fiction when he said that the island named California lay very close to the Terrestrial Paradise ... and just dare to ask those along the south coast exactly where they think that is.

Right: *A small grove of western sycamore at the mouth of Cañada del Capitán at El Capitan State Beach*

■ *Left:* A common sight in the Coast Range, coast live oaks, with their leaning trunks and spreading branches, thrive in Arroyo Bulito on the Hollister Ranch. ■ *Above:* On the Hollister Ranch a rainbow marks the passing of a winter storm over San Augustine Beach near Point Conception. ■ *Overleaf:* Backdropped by the Santa Ynez Mountains, the Santa Barbara Mission was built by Franciscan friars. Often called the Queen of the Missions, it was founded in 1786 to bring Christianity to the Chumash Indians.

■ *Above:* Because of extensive erosion, the palms along the shore at Refugio State Beach are in danger of toppling. As they are considered historically significant, much care is being taken to protect them from further danger. The trees may need to be moved in order to save them. ■ *Right:* Because of the rich and productive ocean resource, the Chumash Indians of the south coast were relatively affluent compared to other groups. Rock art is found in their area, and caves such as the Painted Cave State Historical Park near Santa Barbara remind us of the original Californians.

■ *Left:* The seaside daisy, true to its name, grows just out of reach of the waves on an old dune system in Travertine Cove on San Miguel Island. The westernmost island in Channel Islands National Park, this windswept place is the breeding grounds for more than twenty thousand seals and sea lions. ■ *Above:* The city of Santa Barbara and the Channel Islands of Santa Cruz and Santa Rosa are visible from Camino Cielo, "Highway of the Sky." This road rides the crest of the Santa Ynez Mountains in Los Padres National Forest.

■ *Above: Dudleya greenei* is endemic to San Miguel, Santa Rosa, and Santa Cruz islands. This tough little plant is well adapted to survive the constant battering of wind and weather of the rocky Channel Islands environment. ■ *Right:* Rising out of the sand on San Miguel Island are the forms of "fossil forests," or *caliche.* These former trees and root systems, composed of calcium carbonate, gravel, sand, silt and clay, are part of the most spectacular caliche to be found on the California Channel Islands. In the background, Prince Island, nearly forty acres, is 2.6 miles from the mainland.

■ *Left:* Goldfields cover a coastal dune area near Skunk Point on Santa Rosa Island. This, the second largest of the Channel Islands, was purchased by the National Park Service in 1986 as an addition to the existing Channel Islands National Park. ■ *Above:* There are no visitor facilities on Santa Rosa Island, no campground, no trail, and certainly no traffic jams. Rarely visited, its beaches and tidepools are virtually undisturbed. The beaches are littered with shells, the sand is untracked, and the air is clean. These abalone and wavy and smooth turban shells are near Abalone Rocks.

■ *Above:* An eccentric sand dollar with a single, tiny, pink barnacle washes ashore and settles in the sands of Santa Rosa Island in Channel Islands National Park. Anyone who walks the beaches is familiar with these fragile shells. ■ *Right:* Johnny jump-ups, *Viola pedunculata,* squeeze through a crowd of Torrey pinecones on Santa Rosa Island. The small grove that produced these cones has only about one hundred individual trees. This grove is the smaller of the only two existing Torrey pine groves in the world.

■ *Left:* Because of their isolation from the mainland, all of the Channel Islands harbor endemic plants—species found nowhere else in the world. Eleven such species occur on Santa Cruz Island and are protected by the Nature Conservancy in its Santa Cruz Island Preserve. One of these, the Santa Cruz Island silver lotus, *Lotus argophyllus s. niveus,* is also on the endangered species list.

■ *Above:* Arch Rock is located off East Anacapa Island in Channel Islands National Park. On clear days its distinctive shape can be seen from across the Santa Barbara Channel, fourteen miles away.

■ *Above:* A winter moon sets over Ventura Harbor, the home of the Channel Islands National Park Visitor Center and Park Headquarters. ■ *Right:* The Malibu Pier was built in 1906 and 1907 to bring supplies in and out of the roadless area that is now Malibu. Fredrick Hastings Rindge bought all the land in the area in 1892, hauled the timber in by barge from Santa Monica, and built the pier, one of the original buildings in Malibu. ■ *Overleaf:* The view from Inspiration Point on East Anacapa Island in Channel Islands National Park takes in Middle and West Anacapa islands.

■ *Left:* Santa Catalina Island, more than forty miles away, is clearly visible from the Boney Ridge Trail in the Santa Monica Mountains National Recreation Area. Comprised of pillow basalts, Boney Ridge embraces the highest and most rugged peaks in the Santa Monica Mountains. ■ *Above:* Point Dume, the most prominent headland on the Malibu coast, is accessible at low tide by walking down the beach from Paradise Cove. It was named for Father Dumetz of the Spanish *Misión San Buenaventura,* but Vancouver misspelled the name on his map and it has never been changed.

■ *Above:* Southern California is missing many of the dark and striking offshore seastacks usually associated with the rest of the California coast. But here, at El Matador State Beach west of Malibu, a clearing winter storm shows off these lovely spires. This is the largest concentration of seastacks on the southern California coast. ■ *Right:* A Norris top-shell is wedged between sandstone rocks on Point Dume State Beach in Los Angeles County. These snails spend the majority of their lives grazing upon the kelp plant.

■ *Left:* The magnificent cruise ship RMS *Queen Mary* now makes her home in the Long Beach Harbor, along with thousands of pleasure craft and fishing boats. Once the largest, fastest passenger ship afloat, she now rests, offering the world a chance to tour and view her flashy appointments, while she remains sitting safely tied to the dock. ■ *Above:* Palm trees are in sharp contrast to the mirrored windows of a Long Beach high-rise on Ocean Boulevard. ■ *Overleaf:* The Los Angeles skyline glows in the light of dusk. The *City of the Angels* has always been the star of the southern coast.

■ *Above:* The one million-candlepower Point Vicente Lighthouse has stood on Palos Verdes Peninsula since 1926. It is viewed here from Point Vicente Park, a blufftop park with viewing platforms and a visitor center. ■ *Right:* The Casino, Santa Catalina Island's world-famous landmark, is considered one of the best examples of art deco anywhere. Its theatre and ballroom, both decorated with tile murals, have been popular since its opening in 1929.

■ *Left:* Catalina Clay Products Company at Pebbly Beach was a major industry on Catalina Island from 1927 to 1937, producing brightly glazed tile that is now prized by collectors. Examples, such as this piece at the entrance to what used to be the Aviary, are found throughout the town of Avalon. ■ *Above:* Avalon is the waterfront population center of Catalina Island. Reminiscent of a Mediterranean-style village, it is perched on a hill overlooking Avalon Bay. The Holly Hill House in the foreground and the Casino in the distance are part of the colorful history of Catalina Island.

■ *Above:* One of southern California's valuable ornamentals is the tree aloe. Its bright red flowers, its ability to withstand drought, and its winter blooms make it a favorite for seaside gardens. Several specimens thrive in Heisler Park in Laguna Beach, a lively town famous for its art galleries and shows. ■ *Right:* During the 1920s, fifteen to twenty Japanese families settled in Crystal Cove. When the war broke out, they were sent to internment camps. Though the original families are gone, the homes are considered historically significant and are preserved as part of Crystal Cove State Park.

■ *Left:* Each winter, thousands of western and ringed-billed gulls congregate near Pelican Point in Crystal Cove State Park. This relatively new addition to the State Park System protects three and one-quarter miles of coastline and grassy terraces just south of Newport Bay. ■ *Above:* Southern California coast's warm water and steady winds make it a sailors' paradise. Though Newport Bay and Balboa Island were once busy commercial ports, the bay now overflows with pleasure craft and million-dollar yachts.

■ *Above:* The city of La Jolla is seen in the distance from the Broken Hill Overlook in Torrey Pines State Reserve. The Torrey pine, a sprawling, asymmetrical tree, grows only in California in two places, making it one of our nation's rarest pines. A small stand grows on Santa Rosa Island, off Santa Barbara, and a larger, more accessible grove flourishes amid the eroded badlands of Torrey Pines State Reserve near San Diego. Extensive hiking trails in the reserve wind through several splendid groves of Torrey pines.

■ *Above:* Eroded sandstone badlands line the western perimeter of Torrey Pines State Reserve in San Diego County. These spectacular cliffs in Big Basin, remnants of sand dunes and barrier beaches laid down some twenty million years ago, are examples of the Torrey Formation. The trails through the Torrey pine groves lead to overlooks with numerous panoramic views of the Pacific Ocean.

■ *Above:* The East Corridor of the San Juan Capistrano Mission is just outside the Chapel, considered California's oldest building, and is the state's only remaining church used by Fray Junípero Serra, father of the California missions. San Juan Capistrano is also famous for the swallows that return each March 19 to the mission grounds. ■ *Right:* The western sycamore and coast prickly pear grow in Bell Canyon in the Ronald W. Caspers Wilderness Park. Located in the foothills of the Santa Ana Mountains, the park has an extensive trail system for horseback riders and hikers.

■ *Left:* Common in Baja California but rare in the United States, Shaws agave grows with Torrey pines along the Guy Fleming Trail in Torrey Pines State Reserve. The flowers, whose nectar is enjoyed by hummingbirds, bloom in a "candelabra." ■ *Above:* The second largest city in California, San Diego has it all—an ideal climate, a natural harbor, and a rich, varied history. Discovered in 1542 by Juan Rodriguez Cabrillo, San Diego is the birthplace of California. ■ *Overleaf:* Wind-sculpted Torrey pines repose in the fog along the Guy Fleming Trail in Torrey Pines State Reserve.

■ *Above:* Cabrillo National Monument was named for the explorer who first landed at Point Loma. The Old Point Loma Lighthouse, shown here, was built in 1855, but because it was often obscured by fog, the beacon was replaced in 1891 by a new lighthouse closer to the water at San Diego Bay's entrance. ■ *Right:* Sunset Cliffs Park in Ocean Beach is characterized by steep sandstone cliffs, spectacular ocean views, and numerous pocket beaches. Several trails descend to the beaches, some of which are accessible only at low tide. These sandstone concretions are at Osprey Point.

Recognition, Thanks, And Kudos

It is a flawless California day; the sun has warmed the November morning to perfection, and the air is clear and crisp. We are on a bluff overlooking the Pacific Ocean at Torrey Pines State Reserve near San Diego. Below us, the sea is filled with sparkling waves. Smooth, perfectly formed breakers are coming in slowly, shimmering blue and opaque. Each wave is nearly transparent, and we gaze lazily, transfixed by the sound, letting the motion pull our minds away. We are so hypnotized by the rhythm, so involved in our wave-watching, we forget there's a world going on behind us.

We both noticed them at the same time. Eight dolphins suddenly appeared in the curl, seemingly out of nowhere. We had been so mesmerized by the waves we didn't even see them coming up the coast. These superb swimmers proceeded to put on quite a show; it was a one-ring circus, and we were the only audience. The dolphins leaped out of the water, plunged deep again, and then circled each other quietly. They moved sometimes in unison, sometimes separately, but always they acted as one. Together they played in the translucent water, riding like surfers on an endless wave. Then, as quickly as they had arrived, they disappeared.

We wished we could have thanked those dolphins for their wonderful performance, but they left so quickly we did not get our chance. Since then, though, we continue to acknowledge and thank them each time we have another flawless California day. Each day we spend photographing the California coast is dedicated to the spirit of those eight dolphins.

And now we don't want to let the opportunity to thank the people who helped us with this book slip away. The National Park Service was extremely helpful in assisting us to photograph Channel Islands National Park, and we would especially like to thank Carol Spears, Fred Rodriquez, and all the great rangers for their help. The California Nature Conservancy helped us gain access to Santa Cruz Island and to some of the most spectacular coastal dune areas in the state of California, and we want to thank Harvey Carlson and Ken Wiley for their part.

The personnel at Vandenberg Air Force Base in Lompoc gave us the unique opportunity to see and photograph the splendid shoreline on the base, and we applaud them for their part in preserving this pristine section of coast.

We are grateful to Rod Parsons for helping us photograph the Chumash Painted Cave State Historical Park. And to Gary Strachan at Año Nuevo State Reserve, many thanks for affording us an up-close and personal view of the elephant seals and for sharing his own bird's-eye view of "the green flash."

We would also like to thank some special friends for their help. Lynne Van der Kar has the best place to park a camper in Malibu, and we enjoyed her hospitality. Sue Benech and A. J. Field not only gave us an outstanding ride on a magnificent sailboat, but their combined knowledge of the ocean gave us deeper understanding and love for the place we call home—the coast. These friends are like the dolphins—always a welcome surprise, always special.

LARRY AND DONNA ULRICH